Praying w

GH01032679

Tim Ma

With illustrations by
Taffy
Series Editor: James Jones

 The Bible Reading Fellowship

1

It had been hard work, but it was worth it. The view from the top was stunning: sheer walls of snow plummeted down, birds wheeled in the air below us, and way down, at the foot of the mountain, smooth green Alpine meadows.

On the way back down we met a group of walkers going up. Some of them were just about to turn back—it seemed like too much effort. But we had been to the top, and were able to say 'keep going . . . you won't regret it!'

You've just opened a book called *Praying with Jesus*. And to many people the word 'prayer' sounds like hard work. Indeed, many turn back at the first foothills, convinced it's not much cop. But Jesus has been to the top of the mountain of prayer. He knows the rewards are stunning:

Read Luke 9:28–29, 34–35

Jesus took Peter, John, and James with him and went up a hill to pray. While he was praying, his face changed its appearance, and his clothes became dazzling white . . . A cloud appeared and covered them with its shadow; and the disciples were afraid as the cloud came over them. A voice said from the cloud, 'This is my Son, whom I have chosen—listen to him!'

Learning to pray is just like climbing a mountain. To begin with, it can appear dull and hard work. But the higher you get, the more you can see. And the view from the top is amazing.

So let Jesus teach you to pray. Watch him at prayer. Listen to his teaching.

Follow his example. He'll take you to the mountain top. And if you flag on the way he'll encourage you: 'Keep going . . . you won't regret it!'

Which of these sentences apply to you? Tick as many as you like:

- ☐ I've tried to pray and not got anywhere.
- ☐ I think prayer is boring.
- ☐ I've got lots of questions about prayer, but I'm happy to give it a go.
- ☐ There's probably a lot about prayer I haven't yet discovered.
- ☐ I want Jesus to teach me how to pray.
- ☐ Prayer is the most important thing in my life.
- ☐ I'd love to pray like Jesus, but I don't think I'm good enough.

mountain top

Dear Jesus, you know I'm not perfect.
You know I'm no expert. But I'm
ready to follow. So lead on . . .
teach me to pray. Amen.

First things first

What's the first thing you do in the morning?
☐Fix yourself a drink
☐Watch breakfast TV
☐Shower/shave/make-up, etc.
☐Finish off last night's homework
☐Go back to sleep
☐Other ....

First things are important. The first names you put on your party list show you who your best friends are. The first things you snatch from a blazing building show you what's most important to you. The first things you do each day can set the tone for what's to come.

So have a look at how Jesus kicked off his morning. What strikes you most about it?

Read Mark 1:35–38

> Very early the next morning, long before daylight, Jesus got up and left the house. He went out of the town to a lonely place, where he prayed. But Simon and his companions went out searching for him, and when they found him, they said, 'Everyone is looking for you.' But Jesus answered, 'We must go on to the other villages round here. I have to preach in them also, because that is why I came.'

First things first. Jesus' day began with prayer. He found the right place. He made time for God. For prayer is air—as important as breathing.

Jesus started with prayer. So when the bustle of the day began—Simon hassling him to get back to the people—he didn't have to dance to Simon's tune. He could do what God wanted him to do: press on to other villages and preach there too.

So take a leaf out of Jesus' book. Fairly early in your day, find a quiet corner. Take two or three minutes to be still. Then take several deep breaths, and pray this prayer:

Dear God, Thank you for the gift of life. Gratefully I receive it, and lay it back at your feet. Take me and use me today. Guide me and lead me. Use me to speak and work for you. Amen.

P.S. You find it hard to get up? A famous Christian called David Watson had one alarm clock by his bed and another timed to go off ten minutes later . . . on the landing!

Listening to God

Dale's heart sank. 'Blabber' was cycling towards him. (Blabber's real name was Simon Gough, but people called him 'Blabber' because he never shut up.)

Blabber spotted Dale and got off his bike. He blabbered on about the great goal he'd scored last night. He moaned about his homework. He asked Dale to straighten his back light because it was catching in his spokes.

Eventually Blabber asked Dale how he was getting on at his new school. Dale drew breath, but before he could answer, Blabber was off. 'See you, Dale!'

You and I would run a mile from Blabber. Yet the way he treated Dale is the way we often treat God. We rush up to him, tell him about the good things, moan about the bad things and ask him for lots of other things. And just as he's drawing breath to reply we rush off.

That's not how Jesus prayed. Jesus understood that any conversation involves listening as well as speaking:

 Read Luke 3:21–22

> *After all the people had been baptized, Jesus also was baptized. While he was praying, heaven was opened . . . And a voice came from heaven, 'You are my own dear Son. I am pleased with you.'*

One of the reasons people find prayer boring is that they think it's only about talking. They get no further than 'God bless Auntie Maud'.

Jesus knows different. He knows that God is only too willing to listen to us . . . and only too willing to speak to us too. If only we'd make time to listen.

Listening to God isn't about hearing strange voices. How do you think God might speak to you? Tick as many as you like:

☐ Through the lyrics of singles/albums
☐ Through the Bible
☐ Through sermons in church
☐ Through a strong sense inside
☐ Through 'coincidence'
☐ Through receiving Holy Communion
☐ Through silence
☐ Through other people
☐ Through worshipping God with others
☐ Through nature
☐ Other

Take some time to be still. Then, in your own words, tell God about something that's troubling you. Then make time to listen to what he might say in reply.

P.S. If at first you feel you're getting nowhere in this, don't give up! It's much harder to listen to God than to speak to him. But great rewards await you if you stick at it. Go for it!

From the upper room, Jesus made his way outside the city and into a garden. Here, he'd often prayed. Now, he needed prayer more than ever before.

His friends sank into sleep. But Jesus couldn't rest. He knew his enemies would soon catch up with him. Under cover of darkness he would be arrested. The next day he would suffer a terrible death.

Faced with this terror, listen to how he prays:

 Read Matthew 26:39

> He went a little farther on, threw himself face downwards on the ground, and prayed, 'My Father, if it is possible, take this cup of suffering from me! Yet not what I want, but what you want.'

It took me years to spot it. But once I had, I couldn't forget it: Jesus actually prayed to be let off the cross. The pain and agony he would face the next day caused him to flinch and he prayed 'take this from me!'

But that's only the first half of his prayer. Jesus goes on: *not what I want . . . but what you want.* And when Jesus realized that God's way was the cross, he went there.

We need to learn from Jesus' example. For many people think that prayer is about getting God to do what they want him to do.

In fact, the opposite is true. Praying with Jesus is about getting us to be what God wants us to be. That's the purest prayer we can pray: 'Your will be done.'

But what is God's will for us? Hidden in the word square are ten words that describe what we would like if we really

Your will be done

prayed 'your will be done'. Find each of them, and then tick the word that least describes what you are like:

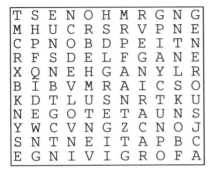

T	S	E	N	O	H	M	R	G	N	G
M	H	U	C	R	S	R	V	P	N	E
C	P	N	O	B	D	P	E	I	T	N
R	F	S	D	E	L	F	G	A	N	E
X	Q	N	E	H	G	A	N	Y	L	R
B	I	B	V	M	R	A	I	C	S	O
K	D	T	L	U	S	N	R	T	K	U
N	E	G	O	T	E	T	A	U	N	S
Y	W	C	V	N	G	Z	C	N	O	J
S	N	T	N	E	I	T	A	P	B	C
E	G	N	I	V	I	G	R	O	F	A

Dear God, sometimes I try to make you do what I want. I'm sorry: please change me. Help me to pray like Jesus. May I be what you want me to be, and do what you want me to do. Amen.

☐ Forgiving
☐ Generous
☐ Kind
☐ Honest
☐ Patient
☐ Involved
☐ Caring
☐ Real
☐ Courageous
☐ Encouraging

Honest to God

Being a teenager can be the most difficult time of your life. You're changing fast. You're trying to get the whole boy/girl thing sorted out. You've got exams to think about. There may well be clashes with your parents.

At church it can be even worse. No one likes your hair. No one likes your clothes. No one likes your music. Everything seems to be arranged for how the adults like it.

Put the whole thing together and it's no surprise you often feel like a churned-up mess inside. But here's the problem, because you're trying to be a Christian. You hear all this stuff about 'peace', and 'prayer' and 'being nice', when all you want to do is scream.

So you've got a choice. You either pretend on the surface that it's all OK. Or you give up the Christian bit because it's just too hard.

But Jesus shows you a third option. He shows you that it's perfectly alright to scream out to God what's really bothering you.

 Read Matthew 27:45–46

> *At noon the whole country was covered with darkness, which lasted for three hours. At about three o'clock Jesus cried out with a loud shout . . . 'My God, my God, why did you abandon me?'*

See? No pretending there. On the cross Jesus felt let down by God. So he told him so, very loudly: *Why did you abandon me?* And loads of people were watching, and heard it. Tut, tut.

Jesus wants you to follow him. He doesn't want you to pretend it's all OK if it's not. If you're churned up inside he wants you to be real with God. So tell him exactly how you feel. After all, he's big enough to take it.

Think about your life. What's most getting you down at the moment? Write it down in one sentence in the box provided. Use code if necessary! When you've written it down, pray the prayer below.

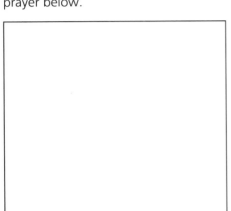

Dear God, you know me perfectly: there's no point pretending with you. You love me perfectly: you understand and you want to help. You know there are times I want to scream. Help me to be real with you. And never let me go. Amen.

6

Hill-top prayer

The town of Brighouse was just about to host the 'God Cares' mission. A team of Christians was shortly to arrive in town, and—through street theatre, concerts and special meetings—tell people the good news about Jesus.

We knew that 'God Cares' would be nothing without prayer. So someone arranged a 'prayer walk'. Fifteen to twenty of us climbed the hills above the town, to look down and pray for all that was about to happen.

We reached a field full of dandelions. The breeze whipped up a cloud of downy seeds and blew them directly towards the town. The link was so clear. So we stopped and prayed: 'Lord God, through "God Cares", send many seeds of your life into Brighouse. Call many people to follow you.'

One reason why people have been tempted to think prayer boring is they get no variety. It's always the same way, in the same place, at the same time. Yawn, yawn.

Jesus was more imaginative about when and where:

 Read Mark 6:46

> After saying goodbye to the people, [Jesus] went away to a hill to pray.

Jesus prayed on hills. He prayed beside rivers. He prayed in boats and houses.

Jesus prayed before important decisions. He prayed during meals. He prayed after hearing good news.

Jesus prayed in gardens. He prayed in the morning. He prayed at night. Prayer was nothing less than the whole of his friendship with God. So any time, any place, would do.

In the left hand side of the box, list all the places in which you've prayed so far. Is the list short? Then in the right hand side, list all the places in which you could pray if you were a bit imaginative.

I JUST DON'T UNDERSTAND IT – THE GARDEN'S FULL OF DANDELIONS!

Dear Jesus, with you it was 'any time, any place, anywhere'. Help me to follow your example. May prayer be for me my whole friendship with God. Amen.

Help! I'm sinking!

He started to panic. All the while he'd been looking at Jesus he'd been fine. But the wind was strong, and the water so deep, that Peter had second thoughts. The waves came up to his ankles, his knees, his waist. There was only one thing for it . . . PRAY!

 Read Matthew 14:30–32

'Save me, Lord!' he cried. At once Jesus reached out and grabbed hold of him and said, 'How little faith you have! Why do you doubt?' They both got into the boat, and the wind died down.

Sometimes life can really get you down. A detention at school . . . exams and tests coming up . . . someone picking on you through no fault of your own. Things pile up and, like Peter, you start to sink.

When that happens, people often forget to pray. All the while things have gone smoothly, it's been fine. At the very moment you most need to pray . . . the habit goes out of the window! No wonder you go on sinking.

So next time things begin to gang up on you, don't forget to pray. It doesn't need to be polished language—Peter only barks out three words—but keep your eyes on Jesus. In his time and in his way he'll lift you up.

On the 1–10 scales, mark how much each of these things makes you sink:

Split up from boyfriend/girlfriend

1 2 3 4 5 6 7 8 9 10

Being bullied at school

1 2 3 4 5 6 7 8 9 10

Can't afford the latest fashions

1 2 3 4 5 6 7 8 9 10

Being teased for going to church

1 2 3 4 5 6 7 8 9 10

Trouble in your family

1 2 3 4 5 6 7 8 9 10

A good friend turning against you

1 2 3 4 5 6 7 8 9 10

Feeling you're no good at anything

1 2 3 4 5 6 7 8 9 10

Being lonely with nobody to talk to

1 2 3 4 5 6 7 8 9 10

Lord Jesus, you know things get tough sometimes, and sometimes I sink. When I start to go under, help me to pray. Please lift me up like you lifted Peter. Amen.

A candle in the darkness

I JUST DON'T KNOW WHAT TO SAY....

Danielle was heartbroken. Her Uncle John and Auntie Karen had only been married two years. Now they'd fallen out in a big way and it looked like curtains.

To make matters worse, Danielle didn't even know what to pray for them. If they made each other so unhappy, perhaps it was best they went their separate ways. But she loved them both so much . . . she really wanted them to get it together.

As she walked along, she saw the church door ajar. She pushed it open. In a dark corner, candles burned. She took one from the box, lit it, and placed it with the others. 'Dear God', she said, 'this is for John and Karen.' She sat for a bit in the quiet, then blinked out into the sunlight again.

You don't always have to use words when you pray. Just look what happened to this woman when she met Jesus:

Read Mark 5:25–29

> There was a woman who had suffered terribly from severe bleeding for twelve years . . . She had heard about Jesus, so she came in the crowd behind him, saying to herself, 'If I just touch his clothes, I will get well.' She touched his cloak, and her bleeding stopped at once; and she had the feeling inside herself that she was healed of her trouble.

There really are times when words aren't enough. Like Danielle you might not know what to pray. Or, like the woman, you might not have the courage to ask for what you need. Or it may well be that you're so aware of God's greatness that no words will do.

At times like that . . . don't say anything. Just be still with God and show him what it is that's troubling you. It may not feel like it at first, but you're praying. After all, the deepest friendships often need the fewest words.

In the box, jot down, or sketch, something that's troubling you: a friend who is poorly; your own worries; someone in your family who is in trouble.

When you've done that, make some time to be alone. Light a candle (you might use an icon as well—a picture of Jesus) and show God what you've written or drawn. Then sit in the quiet with him, in silent prayer.

9 Yes Lord . . .

More than likely she was in her mid teens. She lived in a small village. Everybody knew each other's business. She lived in an age that prized marriage: a woman could be stoned for adultery.

God asked of this young woman something fiercely difficult. She was to become pregnant—before she was married—and have a child in a way that nobody would ever truly understand.

Imagine the thoughts that ran through her mind: 'but I'm engaged to Joseph . . . what will he think? What about the wagging tongues down at the village well?'

Not for nothing was the young Mary worried—after all, we're told that

Joseph wanted to break the engagement. But for her the call of God was more important, and her prayer has become a classic:

 Read Luke 1:38

'I am the Lord's servant,' said Mary; 'may it happen to me as you have said.'

Now it's unlikely that God will send the angel Gabriel to us. God has other ways of showing us what he wants for our lives. Among other things he uses the Bible to show us that. And down the

I'll do it!

☐ *Our love should not be just words and talk; it must be true love, which shows itself in action.*

1 John 3:18

☐ *Be quick to listen, but slow to speak and slow to become angry.*

James 1:19

☐ *Clothe yourselves with compassion, kindness, humility, gentleness, and patience.*

Colossians 3:12

years the Bible has been, for many people, a springboard into prayer. Like this:

Read carefully through these verses from the Bible. Choose just one to focus on. Tick the verse you've chosen.

☐ *Fill your minds with . . . things that are true, noble, right, pure, lovely, and honourable.*

Philippians 4:8

☐ *Do everything possible on your part to live in peace with everybody.*

Romans 12:18

When you've chosen your verse, take some time to be still. Then read your verse, slowly, three times, pausing in between. Enjoy the words: suck them like you would a gobstopper. Then pray Mary's prayer:

I am the Lord's servant. May it happen to me as you have said. Amen.

10 Two journeys

Martin loved cricket. He played all day, and hoped to get picked for the school first team. But he was never as good at real batting as he was in his mind. He kept getting out for low scores, and got really down.

Then his dad noticed a coaching day at the local county ground. It was two bus rides but Martin was determined to get there. When he arrived, he was paired with the county's best batsman—Martin's hero.

The county player showed him a new way to hold his bat. Martin never looked back. Runs flowed for him all season: he was a star, and got into the first team.

Towards the end of the season, he went back to say 'Thank you'. He took two bus rides again when his team was playing at home. He managed to get a word with the star batsman, and thanked him for his help and advice.

Two journeys. One in search of help. The other to say 'Thank you'. See if you can spot them in this reading:

Read Luke 17:11–16, 19

Jesus . . . was met by ten men suffering from a dreaded skin disease. They stood at a distance and shouted, 'Jesus! Master! Take pity on us!' Jesus saw them and said to them, 'Go and let the priests examine you.' On the way they were made clean. When one of them saw that he was healed, he came back, praising God in a loud voice. He threw himself to the ground at Jesus' feet and thanked him . . . And Jesus said to him, 'Get up and go; your faith has made you well.'

Martin's two journeys and the leper's two journeys are very similar. Both went in search of help. Both found it. Both came back to say 'thank you'.

The two journeys can give us a framework for meeting Jesus. Like this:

In the box, write down something that's troubling you at the moment:

Dear Jesus, thank you that you understand. Thank you for giving me your peace and your strength. Amen.

Now make the first journey to Jesus. Imagine you've walked up to him. Tell him what's troubling you. Then imagine him saying to you several times 'peace be with you'. As you breathe in, imagine you're inhaling strength from God.

Then make the second journey. Go to Jesus again and thank him for giving you his strength.

11

Prayer in pain

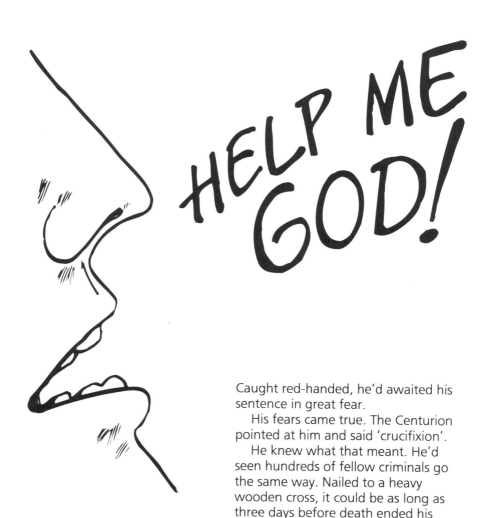

Caught red-handed, he'd awaited his sentence in great fear.

His fears came true. The Centurion pointed at him and said 'crucifixion'.

He knew what that meant. He'd seen hundreds of fellow criminals go the same way. Nailed to a heavy wooden cross, it could be as long as three days before death ended his agony.

But hanging there, as the ordeal started, he recognized the man suffering the same fate beside him. It was Jesus, that wandering preacher from Nazareth. What had he done to deserve this, of all deaths?

Even though he was dying, the thief suddenly realized he believed in Jesus. And even though the pain across his chest was unbearable, he managed to find enough breath to gasp out a prayer:

 Read Luke 23:42–43

> *'Remember me, Jesus, when you come as King!' Jesus said to him, 'I promise you that today you will be in Paradise with me.'*

It's a picture of prayer in pain. You don't have to use fancy words: You don't have to have prayed all your life. Just cry out to Jesus in your pain. He'll hear your prayer.

What strikes you most about the thief's prayer on the cross, and Jesus' response? Tick the sentence that makes most impact on you. Or add your own in the space:

☐ Even though Jesus was dying, the thief still believed he was a King.

☐ Even though Jesus was dying, he still found time to reassure a dying criminal.

☐ Jesus hears the thief's prayer, even though it's only eight words.

☐ Jesus hears the thief's prayer, even though he makes no mention of his crimes.

☐ Jesus promises the thief he'll go to heaven, even though he's only turned to him with hours of life left.

☐ Other . . . .

. . . .

Thank you Jesus. I don't have to use fancy words. I don't have to have been perfect. I don't have to have prayed every day. When I cry to you, you hear me. Thank you.

12

Broken for me

Angus was still coming to terms with it. The exam results were good, but not good enough. A host of dreams came crashing around his ears.

It was still only three months since Molly had lost her husband. She and Walter had done everything together. She missed him so much.

Peter had just heard he'd lose his job next month. He was buying his own house . . . had three children . . . was worried sick.

Angus, and Molly, and Peter found themselves together in church one Sunday. The priest lifted up a loaf of bread, and tore it in half: 'we break this bread to share in the body of Christ'.

As the three of them watched the bread being broken, the penny dropped in their minds. Jesus was broken for them. He was with them in their fears and disappointments.

Here's a story about some other people who were disappointed and afraid. It's only two days since Jesus died. They're walking along the road to a village called Emmaus. Jesus joins them, but they don't recognize him. Saint Luke takes up the story:

Read Luke 24:28–31

> As they came near the village to which they were going, Jesus acted as if he were going farther; but they held him back, saying, 'Stay with us; the day is almost over and it is getting dark.' So he went in to stay with them. He sat down to eat with them, took the bread, and said the blessing; then he broke the bread and gave it to them. Then their eyes were opened and they recognized him.'

Their eyes were opened . . . and they recognized him. That's just what Holy Communion is about. When the bread is broken we remember how Jesus was broken on the cross; when the wine is poured out we remember how his blood was shed. In the Communion service, ask Jesus to help you see him more clearly.

Here's a list of things that Holy Communion means. Tick the ones that you've experienced, or add your own in the space:

☐ Remembering the death of Jesus

☐ Receiving from God

☐ Sharing with each other

☐ Meeting with Jesus

☐ Offering myself to God

☐ Looking forward to heaven

☐ Other . . . .

. . . .

. . . .

Lord Jesus, your disciples prayed 'stay with us', and you answered their prayer. In the service of Holy Communion, help me to know you more clearly, to love you more dearly, and to follow you more nearly. Amen.

13

You can make me clean

His disease was deadly. So he was supposed to keep his distance. He was supposed to live outside the village, and ring a bell to warn people away.

Instead, he came right up to Jesus. He fell on his knees, and prayed:

13

 Read Mark 1:40–42

'If you want to,' he said, 'you can make me clean.' Jesus was filled with pity, and stretched out his hand and touched him. 'I do want to,' he answered. 'Be clean!' At once the disease left the man, and he was clean.

The leper was 'unclean' on the *outside*. His disease would have eaten away at his skin. That's why it's so powerful that Jesus touched him.

But you don't have to have a disease to be 'unclean' on the *inside*. All kinds of things build up inside us . . . wrong thoughts, anger, lies and hate . . . all these things build up inside us and make us 'unclean'. God knows all about those things, but the last thing he wants is to punish us for them. Instead, because he loves us, he wants to set us free. He wants to wash us clean.

But there's something we need to do before he can do that. Like the leper, we need to come to Jesus and ask for help. We need to say 'sorry' for the ways we've let God down, and ask him to make us clean.

It's my experience that God will always do that. Time and again, when I've let the nasty stuff build up inside, he hears my prayer. When I cry out to him, 'Lord if you want to, you can make me clean!' he says to me, 'I do want to . . . be clean.'

Think about your life. And in the box below, write softly, in pencil, some of the things inside you that make you 'unclean'. Choose words from the list if you want to—to get you started. But by all means add your own if you want to:

☐ Jealousy   ☐ Mockery
☐ Hate   ☐ Resentment
☐ Greed   ☐ Bullying
☐ Anger   ☐ Lies
☐ Spite   ☐ Gossip

When you've finished writing in the box, take some time to think about what you've written. Then pray:

Lord, if you want to,
you can make me clean.

Then imagine Jesus saying to you:

I do want to . . . be clean.

Then rub out all you've written in the box, and thank God: he's made you clean!

Know yourself

Mark had all the gear. Flashy sports bag. State of the art racket. Multi-coloured Wimbledon kit.

To speak to him, you'd thing he was the best. Anything you mentioned . . . he'd been there. He'd done it.

The only thing was, he was no good at tennis! All over the school people laughed behind his back. It was all show. Mark thought he was number one. The scoreboard told a different story.

You may have met people like Mark. There's a gap between who they really are, and who they think they are. You wish they'd 'know themselves' better.

One of the best things about asking God to forgive us is that it shows us who we really are. It helps us to 'know ourselves', and stops us pretending to be something we're not. Like Simon Peter:

Read Luke 5:8–10

When Simon Peter saw what had happened, he fell on his knees before Jesus and said, 'Go away from me, Lord! I am a sinful man!' He and the others with him were all amazed at the large number of fish they had caught... Jesus said to Simon, 'Don't be afraid; from now on you will be catching people.'

Jesus helped Simon to 'know himself'. Faced with Jesus' power, he realized he was far from perfect: *Go away from me, Lord! I am a sinful man.*

But Jesus didn't answer his prayer! Simon prayed *Go away from me...* Jesus did the opposite. He called Simon to follow him.

It's just the same for us. When we confess our sins it's not the end of the story. It opens a door for God. He shows us who we are: a sinner in need of forgiveness. He assures us of what

we can be: someone called to serve God, as we get up and follow Jesus.

How well do you 'know yourself'? Score yourself out of ten for each of the following statements:

I sometimes think badly about people of a different race

1   2   3   4   5   6   7   8   9   10

Sometimes I'm two-faced, and run down friends behind their back

1   2   3   4   5   6   7   8   9   10

I sometimes tell lies to get out of tricky situations

1   2   3   4   5   6   7   8   9   10

I sometimes show off to attract members of the opposite sex

1   2   3   4   5   6   7   8   9   10

I sometimes join the crowd in mocking someone weak

1   2   3   4   5   6   7   8   9   10

Dear Jesus, help me not to pretend. Help me to see myself as you see me: in need of forgiveness, but deeply loved by God. Amen.

15

Your sins are
forgiven

Tina was a loner. Everyone knew about what she'd done, and couldn't really forget it. Nobody wanted to sit with her at dinner. Nobody wanted to walk home with her.

Then a new girl, Samantha, joined the class. She didn't know about Tina's past—just saw her as someone lonely. Soon Tina and Samantha were firm friends.

Sometimes the past gangs up on us. Something we've done or said haunts us, and we wish it would go away. What we need then is someone who's not so much concerned with the past as with the present and the future. Someone like Jesus:

Read Luke 7:36–40, 48, 50

A Pharisee invited Jesus to have dinner with him, and Jesus went to his house and sat down to eat. In that town was a woman who lived a sinful life. She . . . brought an alabaster jar full of perfume and stood behind Jesus . . . crying and wetting his feet with her tears. Then she dried his feet with her hair, kissed them, and poured the perfume on them. When the Pharisee saw this, he said to himself, 'If this man really were a prophet, he would know who this woman is who is touching him; he would know what kind of sinful life she lives!' Jesus . . . said to woman, 'Your sins are forgiven . . . Your faith has saved you; go in peace.'

To Jesus, the present and the future are more important than the past. Often, he's only concerned about things in our past in so far as he can forgive us and release us from their power.

That's what 'the sinful woman' discovered. To the Pharisee, the religious leader, she was just somebody with a mucky past. To Jesus she was someone to be forgiven in the present and set free for the future.

What is there in your past for which you long to receive forgiveness? Write it in the box. Use code if necessary.

Then, remembering that prayer is a conversation, say to Jesus:

Lord Jesus, you long to set me free from the past. Please forgive me. Help me to live in the present, and to face the future.

Then imagine Jesus saying to you:

Your sins are forgiven . . . Your faith has saved you; go in peace.

POP!

Arrested at the dead of night, Jesus suffered a mockery of a trial. Not even the false witnesses could agree about which lies to tell about him.

His judge, Pontius Pilate, found him innocent . . . and then pronounced the death sentence. He was whipped and beaten by soldiers who wanted a cheap laugh. Then he carried his cross up a hill outside the city.

There, they nailed him to it, and left him to die. Yet even then, in the agony of crucifixion, Jesus was thinking about the needs of other people. And even then, he prayed for them:

 Read Luke 23:33–34

When they came to the place called 'The Skull', they crucified Jesus there, and the two criminals, one on his right and the other on his left. Jesus said 'Forgive them, Father! They don't know what they are doing.'

Jesus does not expect us to follow where he is not prepared to lead. Having taught us to forgive our enemies, he lived it out. And even when they nailed him to a cross he prayed for them. He asked his father to forgive them.

If we are to pray with Jesus, we need to follow his example. Jesus prayed for his enemies. We who follow him are called to do the same.

Here's a list of words to describe Jesus on the cross. Find all ten, and then tick the word which best sums up Jesus in this moment:

B	A	N	T	G	N	I	V	I	G
R	D	B	R	A	V	E	P	C	T
O	V	D	A	R	M	B	L	R	O
K	E	S	H	N	P	S	O	F	R
E	R	N	T	L	D	B	V	L	T
N	V	Q	O	X	F	O	I	O	U
H	S	I	F	L	E	S	N	U	R
N	Z	H	C	X	A	L	G	E	E
T	E	X	H	A	U	S	T	E	D
G	N	I	V	I	G	R	O	F	C

☐ Brave   ☐ Abandoned
☐ Tortured   ☐ Loving
☐ Forgiving   ☐ Alone
☐ Exhausted   ☐ Broken
☐ Unselfish   ☐ Giving

Lord Jesus, even nailed to the cross, you prayed for your enemies. Help me to follow in your footsteps. Amen.

Forgive them, Father

In the previous unit, we saw how Jesus was able to forgive the people who nailed him to the cross. We recognized that if we are to pray with Jesus, we need to try to be like him.

But we don't always find it easy. Sometimes the things people do to us, say about us, or don't do for us, wound us so deeply that we would be pretending if we said, 'God, I forgive them.'

Jesus understands that we find it difficult, and wouldn't want us to pretend. He knows there are times when we don't even want to forgive, because we've been hurt so badly. He knows that bitterness is like a poison inside.

But when he teaches us to pray, Jesus links very closely the forgiveness we receive from God with the forgiveness we show to others:

 Read Matthew 6:12

> *Forgive us the wrongs we have done, as we forgive the wrongs that others have done to us . . .*

See? In the Lord's Prayer we ask God to forgive us in the same way that we forgive others. Awesome words . . . especially if we find we really can't forgive someone.

So have a think. Who do you need to forgive? Write their initials in the space in the prayer.

Now ask yourself: 'Can I pray this prayer?'

Father God, I forgive . . . . . I release to you all the anger I feel towards him/her. Help me sincerely to want what is best for him/her. And help me to forget it ever happened. Amen.

If you can, then pray the prayer out loud in a private place. If you can't, then don't. God doesn't want you to pretend. Instead, if you don't even want to forgive the person, trace out these three steps:

1. Recognize that God is as angry as you are about the hurt you've suffered.

2. Recognize, though, that God still wants to forgive the person who hurt you.

3. Even if you can't forgive the person yourself, ask God to forgive them. Pray these words to Jesus:

Forgive . . .
as we
forgive

Father, forgive them. Amen.

P.S. You won't find this easy, but whenever you think of the person, try praying with Jesus 'Father, forgive them'. Until one day you can forgive them yourself.

18 Your kingdom come

Alfredo grows bananas in Haiti. He works hard all day, but hardly earns enough to support his young family. Instead, other people get rich on Alfredo's work: as his bananas make their way to your supermarket, middle-men slap profits on them. They become rich. Alfredo remains poor.

Gita is eight. It's a long walk from her Bangladeshi village to the nearest water supply. She often makes the journey, bringing back water for family. Even then, the water she brings back is likely to carry disease. Meanwhile, the rich nations of the earth continue to spend billions of pounds on new weapons.

Whu is a Chinese Christian, hosting house group meetings in her home. She was told by the authorities to stop holding the meetings. When she refused she was sentenced to two years in prison.

Hold Alfredo, Gita, and Whu in your mind as you hear Jesus teaching you to pray:

 Read Matthew 6:9–10

> *This, then, is how you should pray: 'Our Father in heaven: May your holy name be honoured; may your Kingdom come; may your will be done on earth as it is in heaven.'*

Does it honour God's holy name that the middle-men get rich while Alfredo remains poor? Is it God's will that Whu should be imprisoned for her faith? Is it the kingdom of God where billions of pounds are spent on weapons, not water?

Of course not. God's anger burns when his name is dishonoured. We who love God should be angry too. But our anger should drive us to action, and to prayer. When we hear about the injustice of the world let's pray 'your kingdom come' . . . and then do something about it.

Imagine you are God. Out of love you made the world. What are some of the things you see in the world that anger and sadden you? Write them in the left-hand column:

Now, in the right-hand column, write the opposite of each thing you wrote in the left-hand column (e.g. 'war'— 'peace'). The things in the right-hand column are the things we should be praying for when we say 'your kingdom come'.

Our Father in heaven, may your holy name be honoured for Alfredo. May your kingdom come for Gita. May your will be done for Whu. Amen.

19

Outside the town of Nazareth were fields. There, the people of the town would sow their own crops, and wait hopefully for them to grow. If the harvest was good, the whole town would celebrate. If not, the people knew they faced a winter of hunger.

The young Jesus, growing up in Nazareth, would have seen the sowing and the harvesting time and again. He knew that the harvest was a matter of life or death. That's why he taught his followers to pray.

 Read Matthew 6:11

| *Give us today the food we need.*

How different things are in England nearly two thousand years later. We push our trolleys down the supermarket aisles. Without pausing to wonder at the goodness of God we pile it up: bread, cornflakes, peaches. All winter long, when nothing grows in our country, the shelves are still fully stocked. And we go on piling high the trolleys, with no thought about how the goods got here.

So it's very tempting to ignore Jesus' prayer asking God for 'the food we need'. But if we do, we are the poorer. For Jesus' prayer is powerful for our age. In two ways:

First, in the age of the deep freeze and cling film, Jesus' prayer reminds us where it all comes from. It comes from God, the generous giver. We should not take it all for granted, but celebrate the one who put it there.

And secondly, Jesus' prayer reminds us that all over the world there are still people like the farmers of Nazareth in his own day: growing their own food. Doomed if the harvest fails.

So celebrate the food you have, and then pray for God to supply the needs of the poor. In the box below, list your top ten favourite foods:

Thank you, God, for:
1 . . . .
2 . . . .
3 . . . .
4 . . . .
5 . . . .
6 . . . .
7 . . . .
8 . . . .
9 . . . .
10 . . . .

Once you have your list, if you're in a group, take it in turns to see if you can read out the contents of your box in one breath. If you're on your own, make it your own prayer to God, then pray:

Our daily bread

Dear God, thank you for supplying all my needs. Forgive me when I take my food for granted. And hear me as I cry to you for the hungry of the earth. Amen.

Before the war, Pierre's orchard was his pride and joy. The apple harvest was the best part of the year. The whole village came and helped, and there was music, dancing and laughter.

Now, ahead of the invading army, Pierre's village was a ghost town. Everyone had fled. It would have broken Pierre's heart to see this harvest: over-ripe apples dropping one by one to rot in the long grass.

A harvest without workers. That's just what Jesus saw on his preaching tour of Galilee:

 Read Matthew 9:35–38

Jesus went round visiting all the towns and villages. He taught in the synagogues, preached the Good News about the Kingdom, and

Send out workers

healed people with every kind of disease and sickness. As he saw the crowds, his heart was filled with pity for them, because they were worried and helpless, like sheep without a shepherd. So he said to his disciples, 'The harvest is large, but there are few workers to gather it in. Pray to the owner of the harvest that he will send out workers to gather in his harvest.'

The harvest that Jesus spoke of was not a harvest of apples. It was a harvest of lives. The people he met had seen God at work. They wanted to know more about him. There was a whole harvest of people waiting to follow Jesus. But

he couldn't 'harvest' them on his own. He needed fellow workers. So he told his followers to pray for workers to gather in his harvest.

It's just the same today. All over the world, in the lives of countless people, God is at work. Many of them will become ripe, today, to hear more about God. But without workers to help them, many may pass that point, and drift away. It's urgent business, says Jesus. So pray, today, for more workers.

Who do you know who's already working with God to help people know more about Jesus? Write their names alongside each category:

CHRISTIAN ROCK SINGER

YOUTH WORKER

CHURCH MINISTER

CHRISTIAN TEACHER

EVANGELIST

SUNDAY SCHOOL TEACHER

OTHER . . . .

Dear God, I pray for every person I've named. Give them strength as they work to tell people about Jesus. And send out more workers into your harvest. Amen.

21

The good father's gifts

Derek's lorry thundered down the dark motorway. He was miles from home. On the dashboard, pictures of his children. David was fourteen last week, Nicola nearly twelve.

Rubbing his eyes, Derek was glad to see the next services. He turned off the motorway and got a stiff black coffee. Then he went into the shop. He got a king size Mars for David, and a copy of Nicola's favourite comic. Only little things, but enough to show Derek's children he was thinking about them.

Any good father is often thinking about his children. He wants to show them his love, and do what's best for them. Jesus started with that picture when he wanted to tell us more about God:

 Read Luke 11:11–13

Would any of you who are fathers give your son a snake when he asks for fish? Or would you give him a scorpion when he asks for an egg? Bad as you are, you know how to give good things to your children. How much more, then, will the Father in heaven give the Holy Spirit to those who ask him!

Almighty God is not just any old father. He is the best parent there will ever be. The Bible is full of pictures of God caring for us as if we were his children.

This is one such picture. A human father knows how to give his children gifts. How much more, then, will God give us his gifts. And not just any gift, says Jesus, but the gift of his Holy Spirit: the presence of God inside us.

P.S. If you're enjoying this book, you might like to know that there's more about God's Holy Spirit in *The Spirit of Jesus*, another book in this series.

Here's a list of things the Holy Spirit does in our lives. Which of these would you like him to do for you? Tick as many as you like:

☐ He gives us power to follow Jesus.

☐ He adopts us as God's sons and daughters.

☐ He makes us clean inside.

☐ He makes us more like Jesus.

☐ He guides us through our lives.

☐ He makes God feel very close.

☐ He fills our lives with God's love.

Heavenly Father, Jesus taught me to ask you for the Holy Spirit. I gladly do so. Fill my life with your Spirit. Amen.

Flying into Pakistan, the aeroplane crashed in the mountains. The missionary family on board were killed instantly. They never got to start their work overseas.

For some reason, they ganged up on the Catholic mission. Before the violence had stopped, all the nuns had been hacked to death. They died in Africa, and never saw home again.

The love of God grips people. Many of them leave homes, jobs and family to serve him overseas. Some of them never return. The dangers they face gang up on them. Their mission for God ends in death.

But both the missionary family and the Catholic nuns had people praying for them. So were those prayers unanswered? No—because no one, not even the devil, could take away their friendship with God or their home in heaven.

That's what Jesus meant when he told us to pray for each other. He taught us to pray that our friendship with God might be kept safe:

 Read John 17:9–15

I pray for them . . . Holy Father! Keep them safe by the power of your name . . . While I was with them, I kept them safe by the power of your name . . . I protected them, and not one of them was lost . . . I gave them your message, and the world hated them, because they do not belong to the world, just as I do not belong to the world. I do not ask you to take them out of the world, but I do ask you to keep them safe from the Evil One.

So find out all you can about someone who is serving God overseas. It might be your church's link missionary, or someone you've read about, or heard about at school. Fill in their details on this chart:

Name: .... Base country: ....

One thing to pray for missionary: ....

....

One thing to pray for country: ....

....

One thing to thank God for: ....

....

Write on God's hand the name of the missionary you're praying for.

Keep them safe

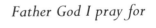

Father God I pray for

. . . . .

Thank you that he/she has answered your call and is serving you overseas. Please keep him/her safe. But above all, don't let anyone snatch him/her out of the Father's hand. Amen.

P.S. If you've prayed for someone overseas, why not write and tell them so. You'll make their day!

The visitor from Mars scratched his head. The language de-coder crackled into life again. 'Let's . . . get . . . this . . . straight', puzzled the alien: 'Tell . . . me . . . again . . .' So you do . . .

'You see, first there were just Christians. Then Western Christians fell out with Eastern Christians. The Western ones were "Catholics" and the Eastern ones were "Orthodox".

'Then the "Protestants" fell out with the "Catholics", and then the "Protestants" fell out with each other. Some became "Anglicans", others "Baptists", others "Methodists". Then some "Methodists" fell out with other "Methodists" and became "Primitive Methodists". Then . . .'—but the Martian interrupts:

'I'm . . . sorry . . . I . . . thought . . .

you . . . said . . . this . . . Christian . . . thing . . . was . . . about . . . LOVE!'

Anybody looking in on the history of the Church would be puzzled. It's supposed to be all about love. But we keep falling out with each other! That's why Jesus prayed that we may be one:

 Read John 17:20–23

> I pray not only for them, but also for those who believe in me because of their message. I pray that they may all be one . . . So that the world will believe that you sent me. I gave them the same glory you gave me, so that they may be one just as you and I are one: I in them and you in me, so that

Make them one

they may be completely one, in order that the world may know that you sent me and that you love them as you love me.

How much do you know about the other churches in your area? Fill in as much of the chart as you can.

	Name of church	Minister's name	Member of congregation
Anglican			
Baptist			
Catholic			
House Church			
Methodist			
United Reformed			

Spend some time praying quietly for each church and individual you've named. Then pray this prayer . . .

Father, help us to be one, just as you and Jesus are one. Help us to work together so that others may see your love in us. Amen.

So you're full of good ideas about praying. The only thing is . . . where are you going to do it?

The kitchen's out, for starters: Mum's cooking the tea, and has the radio on full blast. Dad's just come in from work and is slumped in the living room watching a video of last night's boxing.

Hmmm. You climb the stairs. Your bedroom's out—you share it with your brother and he's zapping aliens on the computer. And in their bedroom, down the landing, the twins are fighting tooth and nail.

There's only one thing for it. Tucking your copy of *Praying with Jesus* under your arm, you sneak into the loo and snap shut the bolt: 'Engaged'!

It's obvious, isn't it. If you're going to get any praying done, you've got to find a place to do it.

 Read Matthew 6:6

> When you pray, go to your room, close the door, and pray to your Father, who is unseen. And your Father, who sees what you do in private, will reward you.

Go to your room, said Jesus. But as we've seen, that might well be a problem. So think about your family and your home. When is the place quietest—the best time to think about praying? Think about the rooms in your house, and when they're used. Which one is most suitable? Jot your ideas down on the chart:

What time is best?
What room is best?

Dear Jesus, you best know how easy or difficult it is to find some peace in my house. But help me to find the right time and the right place to be alone with you. Amen.

Where shall I pray?

It's a glorious day. The sun is beating down. You're swimming in the clear, blue sea. Huge breakers sweep in from the ocean. You catch one, and like a human surfboard it billows you towards the beach.

You reach the shallows and stagger to your feet. The sun has filled the water with a million diamonds. It's one of the best moments of your life. So you look into the sky and bellow at the top of your voice . . . 'Thank you God!'

Lots of Christians seem to think that to be truly 'praying', your prayer's got to be really long, and really heavy. I wonder why that is. Especially as Jesus said:

Read Matthew 6:7–8

When you pray, do not use a lot of meaningless words, as the pagans do, who think that their gods will hear them because their prayers are long. Do not be like them.

Now that's interesting. Jesus said don't go on and on and on. And don't use long prayers. I wonder how many people have spotted that.

Saint Benedict did. He said 'let your prayers be brief and pure'. That doesn't mean 'pray less'. It means 'when you pray, say less, and connect with God more'.

Dear God, thank you. Amen.

So don't be put off by long and complicated prayers. Next time you stand up in the smashing surf and from your heart shout 'Thank you God' . . . you're praying with Jesus.

Here are some other short prayers. Unjumble the words, and write them in the space provided.

VOGFIRE EM, DROL! . . . .

EKAT YM FELI . . . .

REDA DOG, LEPH! . . . .

LILF EM, YOHL IPRIST . . . .

VESA HET ROPO! . . . .

Brief and pure

The air was thick with curses. The chain on Liam's bike was snagged with the gear mechanism. He'd tried everything to work it loose, without success. Eventually his patience snapped, and the spanner flew across the garage.

Sitting in the living room, Dad was wondering what to do for the best. He'd spotted the problem with Liam's chain, and knew he could fix it. But . . . should he muscle in? Wasn't it better to let Liam work it out for himself?

He decided to leave it up to Liam. He knew where his Dad was. If he came and asked for help, of course he'd give it gladly.

He'd just decided this, when he heard footsteps through the kitchen. It was Liam. 'Dad, can you give us a hand with the bike, please?' 'Of course.'

Hold that story in your mind as Jesus teaches you to pray:

Your Father knows

Read Matthew 6:7–8

When you pray, do not use a lot of meaningless words, as the pagans do, who think that their gods will hear them because their prayers are long. Do not be like them. Your Father already knows what you need before you ask him.

Liam's story, and Jesus' words, taken together, show us why we don't need to go on and on in our prayers: our Father knows what we need before we ask.

So why do we have to ask? Why doesn't God just give us what we need? It's because that's how you relate to a baby . . . and God wants us to 'grow up into Christ'. Liam needed to wrestle with the problem himself first. It showed him he needed help. It prepared him to learn from watching Dad do it . . . so that next time Liam could do it himself.

So think about your life at the moment. What do you really need? Jot those things down in the box provided:

GOD KNOWS I NEED . . .

Father, you know me better than I know myself. You know what I need before I ask. Don't give me things just because I want them. Give me the things you know I really need. Amen.

Trust me

The promising young gymnast was overjoyed. She'd won a scholarship to study with the Olympic champion.

But now she was in her first session she wasn't so sure. The bar was high . . . the mat a long way down.

The voice of the coach was reassuring: 'Nikki, just swing yourself round the bar and let go. I'll sort you out if it goes wrong. Just trust me!'

To go further in her gymnastics, Nikki has to learn to trust her coach. She wouldn't do anything that would put her pupil at risk. She only wants the best for Nikki.

You and I are not training for Olympic gold—we're learning to pray with Jesus. But just like Nikki, we will only grow in prayer when we learn to trust the one who oversees us.

 Read Luke 12:22–31

'And so I tell you not to worry . . . Can any of you live a bit longer by worrying about it? If you can't manage even such a small thing, why worry about the other things? . . . How little faith you have! So don't be all upset, always concerned about what you will eat and drink . . . Your Father knows that you need these things. Instead, be concerned with his Kingdom, and he will provide you with these things.'

Jesus' words paint a picture of the God we can trust. He knows our needs. He wants what is best for us, even if at times it doesn't seem like it.

So let trust in God be the safety-mat under all your prayers. Tell him about your fears, your worries and your needs, but deep down be full of trust. Trust that God, like Nikki's coach, is rooting for you and only wants the best for you.

What things worry you at the moment? Jot them down in the box provided:

Which of those worries could you yourself do something about, to help you worry less? Underline them, and think about what you could do to ease the worry.

Are your other worries beyond your control? Don't let them eat away at you. Let them take you to God in prayer. And then trust—trust that in God's hands it will work out one day.

Dear God, sometimes it feels like I'm on a high bar, and about to drop off. But help me to trust in you: to trust that even if I fall, you'll be there to catch me. Amen.

28
Thank you, sorry, please

Sometimes Jesus told stories to help us learn more about prayer. Here's one of them:

Read Luke 18:9–14

> 'Once there were two men who went up to the Temple to pray: one was a Pharisee, the other a tax collector. The Pharisee stood apart by himself and prayed, "I thank you, God, that I am not greedy, dishonest, or an adulterer, like everybody else. I thank you that I am not like that tax collector over there. I fast two days a week, and I give you a tenth of all my income." But the tax collector stood at a distance and would not even raise his face to heaven, but beat on his breast and said, "God, have pity on me, a sinner!" I tell you,' said Jesus, 'the tax collector, and not the Pharisee, was in the right with God when he went home.'

Jesus' story means lots of things. It's about being real with God. It's about not being full of self-importance. It's about asking God for forgiveness.

But it's also about the words we use when we pray. The Pharisee's prayer was long and full of fine

YEA VERILY AS THOU DOEST KNOW I AM THY FIN

phrases, but God didn't hear him. His prayer was a boast! It was all about what a fine religious person he was.

The tax collector used simple, everyday words. And they came from the heart—they were a cry for help. So God heard him: he *was in the right with God when he went home.*

So here's how three simple, everyday words can help us to pray:

Look at the chart. In the left hand column you'll find three simple, everyday words or phrases: 'thank you', 'sorry' and 'please'. In the middle column you'll see an example of how to use those words in prayer. Based on that example, write your own simple prayer in the right hand column.

Dear God, thank you that I don't need to use special language when I talk to you. I'm sorry for the times I've been put off you by other people's prayers. Please help me to be real with you when I pray. Amen.

Thank you	THANK YOU FOR MY FAMILY	. . . .
Sorry	I'M SORRY FOR THE TIMES I LOSE MY TEMPER	. . . .
Please	PLEASE MAKE ME A MORE PATIENT PERSON	. . . .

GIFTS... MY GENEROUS WITHOUT CANST DO NAUGHT AND THOU

T AND MOST GRACIOUS SUPPLICANT AND

When I was sixteen I was part of a team that tackled the Ten Tors expedition on Dartmoor. Ten Tors is organized by the army. It involves teams of six walking to ten checkpoints on hilltops ('Tors'), sleeping out for a night on the moor, and carrying all their equipment into the bargain.

The six of us trained for months. We did training walks on the moor. We filled our rucksacks with boulders and climbed steep hillsides. At the end of it all we'd never been so fit: we covered forty-five miles of moorland in little over a day.

What we discovered in the process is the value of being in a team. Each took it in turns to encourage the others. Each of us flagged from time to time and was urged on by team-mates.

We could never have done it on our own. We needed to be part of a team. And Jesus, too, knows the benefit of teamwork—in prayer:

 Read Matthew 18:19–20

> *'I tell you . . . whenever two of you on earth agree about anything you pray for, it will be done for you by my Father in heaven. For where two or three come together in my name, I am there with them.'*

Jesus didn't just say 'shut the door and pray in private'. He encouraged us to pray in teams. The value is enormous. Each member of the team has their

Come together
in my name

own way of speaking about God. Each member of the team brings their own prayer concerns to the group. Put them together and you often have a powerful combination.

So who do you know that you could form a prayer team with? Jot their names in the top half of this box:

In the bottom half, jot down some of the things you might pray for together.

Lord Jesus, thank you that you call us into teams. It's sometimes a struggle on my own. Please give me other people to pray with. Amen.

Never give up

One April day in Lebanon, John McCarthy, a television journalist, was kidnapped. His captors took him to a secret location. It would be over five years before he was freed.

Meanwhile, back in England, McCarthy's girlfriend, Jill Morrell, began to campaign on his behalf. She formed the 'Friends of John McCarthy', and worked round the clock for his release. Countless petitions were handed to politicians, demanding that they do more to secure his release.

And finally, one August day in England, what they had worked so hard to achieve finally happened. John McCarthy walked off an aeroplane a free man.

See if you can spot the similarities between Jill Morrell and the woman in this story:

Read Luke 18:1–5

Jesus told his disciples a parable to teach them that they should always pray and never become discouraged. 'In a certain town there was a judge who neither feared God nor respected people. And there was a widow . . . who kept coming to him and pleading for her rights, saying, "Help me against my opponent!" For a long time the judge refused to act, but at last he said to himself, "Even though I don't fear God or respect people, yet because of all the trouble this widow is giving me, I will see to it that she gets her rights."'

Sometimes the things we pray for happen very quickly. At other times, it can be years before we see what we hoped for. That's why Jesus told his story about the widow. Like Jill Morrell, she went on and on asking for her rights. And, eventually, both women got what they longed for.

So think about what's happening in the world at the moment. In the box, write something you'd love to see happen, but which you fear will take a long time to achieve (e.g. 'world peace'):

Now start praying for what you've written to take place. Go on and on and on praying for it. Never give up. And one day, like Jill Morrell, you may have cause to celebrate.

Lord Jesus, you teach me to pray and never give up. Help me in the project I've taken on. Give me stickability. Help me to pray and pray until justice is done. Amen.

Charged UP

All week long James had known. At any point he could have stuck his batteries in the re-charger. He'd decided to risk it, and now wished he hadn't.

His seven-hour train journey had just begun. And here, stuck in some blasted industrial estate, his personal stereo had packed in. The batteries had finally given up the ghost.

James winced. Down the carriage a baby was crying. Across the aisle a little boy was whining for more crisps. Disaster!

Jesus knows that human beings are a bit like batteries. We can only go on so long. We can only give out so much. There comes a time when we need to rest, and to receive from God.

So where a battery needs to go into the re-charger, we need to *remain united* to Jesus:

Read John 15:4–5

> 'Remain united to me, and I will remain united to you. A branch cannot bear fruit by itself; it can do so only if it remains in the vine. In the same way you cannot bear fruit unless you remain in me. I am the vine, and you are the branches. Those who remain in me, and I in them, will bear much fruit; for you can do nothing without me.'

Jesus' promise is that if we *remain united* to him, we will *bear much fruit*. Put another way, that means that if we constantly draw on the power of God he will help us to live a 'full' life.

The thing is . . . how do we draw on the power of God? Perhaps this chart will help.

Morning	
Afternoon	
Evening	

You'll see a chart for 'morning', 'afternoon' and 'evening'. As far as you're able to, jot down in the right-hand column what you'll be doing at each stage of the day. If you're doing this unit first thing in the morning, fill in the chart for the day ahead. If it's later on in the day, fill it in for tomorrow.

Then, if you can, take this book with you through the day. Take some time first thing, at lunchtime, and before the evening, to ask Jesus to 'remain' with you. You don't have to spend hours on it. Just ask Jesus for his strength at each point of the day.

Lord Jesus, throughout today, be with me. Help me to remain united to you. Fill my life with your life. Amen.

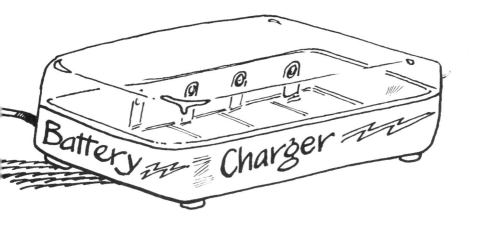

What next?

The *Following Jesus* Series

If you have enjoyed using *Praying with Jesus*, you might like to look at other titles in the series. All are available singly or in packs of 10 copies.

Following Jesus—31 units which explore the basics of the Christian faith.

Serving Jesus—31 units which encourage us to serve Jesus in the world today.

The Power of Jesus—28 units which consider the power of Jesus as seen in the seven signs in John's Gospel.

Picturing Jesus—28 units which consider the seven 'I Am' sayings in John's Gospel—the pictures which Jesus used to illustrate and show who he was: 'I am the Good Shepherd', 'I am the Vine', 'I am the Bread of Life', 'I am the Way, the Truth and the Life', 'I am the Light of the World', 'I am the Resurrection and the Life', 'I am the Gate'.

Stories by Jesus—31 units which consider ways Jesus used parables to illustrate his teaching and shows how they still relate to and challenge us 2,000 years later.

Surprised by Jesus—31 units which consider ways in which Jesus surprised people by what he said and what he did.

The Spirit of Jesus—31 units which consider the Holy Spirit: the story of the Spirit, pictures of the Spirit and the Holy Spirit and you.

The Teaching of Jesus—29 units consider the teaching of Jesus in the Sermon on the Mount (Matthew 5–7).

The final three volumes in the series, *Sent by Jesus*, *The Touch of Jesus* and *The Cross of Jesus* will be published in early 1995.

All titles in the series are illustrated throughout by Taffy, and are available now from all good Christian bookshops, or in case of difficulty from BRF, Peter's Way, Sandy Lane West, Oxford, OX4 5HG.

If you would like to know more about the full range of Bible reading notes and other Bible reading group study materials published by BRF, write and ask for a free catalogue.